AN EDITION OF MILES HOGARDE'S *A MIRROURE OF MYSERIE*

Before you start to read this book, take this moment to think about making a donation to punctum books, an independent non-profit press,

@ https://punctumbooks.com/support/

If you're reading the e-book, you can click on the image below to go directly to our donations site. Any amount, no matter the size, is appreciated and will help us to keep our ship of fools afloat. Contributions from dedicated readers will also help us to keep our commons open and to cultivate new work that can't find a welcoming port elsewhere. Our adventure is not possible without your support.

Vive la Open Access.

Fig. 1. Hieronymus Bosch, *Ship of Fools* (1490–1500)

AN EDITION OF MILES HOGARDE'S *A MIRROURE OF MYSERIE*. Copyright © 2021 by Sebastian Sobecki. This work carries a Creative Commons BY-NC-SA 4.0 International license, which means that you are free to copy and redistribute the material in any medium or format, and you may also remix, transform and build upon the material, as long as you clearly attribute the work to the authors (but not in a way that suggests the authors or punctum books endorses you and your work), you do not use this work for commercial gain in any form whatsoever, and that for any remixing and transformation, you distribute your rebuild under the same license. http://creativecommons.org/licenses/by-nc-sa/4.0/

First published in 2021 by punctum books, Earth, Milky Way.
https://punctumbooks.com

ISBN-13: 978-1-953035-53-0 (print)
ISBN-13: 978-1-953035-54-7 (ePDF)

DOI: 10.21983/P3.0316.1.00

LCCN: 2021936609
Library of Congress Cataloging Data is available from the Library of Congress

Book design: Vincent W.J. van Gerven Oei
Cover photograph: "Cloude Gate" by Anish Kapoor. Photograph by Peter Miller, Chicago, September 3, 2016.

spontaneous acts of scholarly combustion

HIC SVNT MONSTRA

Sebastian Sobecki

An Edition of Miles Hogarde's
A Mirroure of Myserie

p.

Contents

An Edition of Miles Hogarde's
A Mirroure of Myserie
(San Marino, CA, Huntington Library, MS HM 121)

Introduction · 13

Text · 19

Bibliography · 61

Acknowledgments

My deepest gratitude goes to the Huntington Library for having elected me to an Andrew W. Mellon Foundation Short-Term Fellowship in 2015. The Library's generous assistance allowed me to study and transcribe Huntington Library MS HM 121, the sole known copy of Miles Hogarde's *Mirroure of Myserie*.

Without Eileen Joy and Vincent W.J. van Gerven Oei's enthusiastic support this project would not have seen the light of day. I am grateful to punctum books for agreeing to take on this edition.

INTRODUCTION

An Edition of Miles Hogarde's *A Mirroure of Myserie* (San Marino, CA, Huntington Library, MS HM 121)

Miles Hogarde (also Huggarde) was one of the most remarkable public figures during Mary I's brief reign. The Queen's shoemaker by appointment, the autodidact Hogarde became the leading pamphleteer of the Counter-Reformation. Little else is known about his life. He first appears as hosier to the Queen on 25 November 1553, and nothing is known about him after 1557.[1]

Of his nine known works, only *A Mirroure of Myserie* — his last substantial text — never saw print. It survives in a single manuscript, San Marino, CA, Huntington Library, MS HM 121. There exist relatively few references to this work, and only fragments of it have been quoted by modern scholarship. The sole discussion of this poem amounts to some two pages in Joseph Martin's 1981 book *Religious Radicals in Tudor England*.[2] Despite Hogarde's role as the 'best of Roman Catholic propagandists' at

---

[1] C. Bradshaw, 'Huggarde, Miles (fl. 1533–1557)', in *Oxford Dictionary of National Biography* (Oxford: Oxford University Press, 2004).

[2] Joseph W. Martin, *Religious Radicals in Tudor England* (London: Continuum, 1989), 103–5. The chapter was first published as 'Miles Hogarde: Artisan and Aspiring Author in Sixteenth-Century England', *Renaissance Quarterly* 34, no. 3 (October 1, 1981): 359–83, but without the material on *A Mirroure of Myserie*.

the time and as the 'most prolific Marian author',[3] this 900-line dream poem remains inaccessible to contemporary scholarship.

There are good reasons for editing this poem now. First, the ongoing re-evaluation of the Henrician reformation and its legacy has paved the way for renewed interest in the Mid-Tudor period and the polemical debates during Mary's reign.[4] Since the religious controversies of the Henrician years spilled over into the Mid-Tudor years, scholars are beginning to see the reign of Mary not as a hiatus in the Protestant historiography of sixteenth-century England but as a significant period for controversialist writings.[5] Second, there is growing awareness of the social impact of Mid-Tudor writers who enjoyed little or no formal education. Hogarde is an example of a new class of writers that emerged during the 1540s and '50s: literate men and women from non-traditional backgrounds who never went to one of the universities or the Inns of Court. I have argued elsewhere that this group of writers stood behind the various rebellions of 1549.[6] What made these insurgencies so formidable was not so much the sophisticated dialogue with the authorities into which the rebels entered, but the active support lent by 'lernyd men' and scriveners. For all their social and political significance, these risings exemplified the transformative energies released by access to basic education. By offering their intellectual capital to popular movements, such 'lernyd men' turned local riots into

---

[3] Martin, *Religious Radicals in Tudor England*, 103–5.

[4] See, for instance, Greg Walker, *Writing under Tyranny: English Literature and the Henrician Reformation* (Oxford: Oxford University Press, 2005); Brian Cummings and James Simpson, *Cultural Reformations: Medieval and Renaissance in Literary History* (Oxford: Oxford University Press, 2010).

[5] Recent examples of this trend are Susan Doran and Thomas S. Freeman, eds., *Mary Tudor: Old and New Perspectives* (London and New York: Palgrave Macmillan, 2011) and Vivienne Westbrook and Elizabeth Evenden, *Catholic Renewal and Protestant Resistance in Marian England* (London: Routledge, 2016).

[6] Sebastian Sobecki, *Unwritten Verities: The Making of England's Vernacular Legal Culture, 1463–1549* (Notre Dame: University of Notre Dame Press, 2015).

political movements that threatened Tudor elites. A good example of this phenomenon is Nicholas Moore. Andy Wood describes him as 'a man with legal training' from Colchester who had made a habit of lending his abilities to rebellious causes.[7] Being neither 'studyed, lerned, nor experienced in the commen lawes of the Realme', Moore had 'nevertheles of late tyme taken uppon hym to be aswell a commen councellor in very many and divrs suts depending [...] in the Kyngs honorable Coort of his Chauncery, as a commen councellor and a commen Atturney before the bayliffs of the said Borough'.[8] I would like to think that Hogarde was another such 'lernyd man'. The son of a hosier with no schooling, he produced sophisticated and polished works of religious polemic.

A Mirroure of Myserie is a dream poem, consisting of a brief prose address and 833 lines of verse. The poem begins with a preface to Mary written in eight rhyme-royal stanzas, followed by a prologue in twelve cross-rhymed quatrain stanzas. The poem itself is written in 111 rhyme-royal stanzas. The poem's opening borrows heavily from the fourteenth-century dream vision *Piers Plowman*: in Hogarde's work the Dreamer stands on a hill overlooking the destruction of Sodom and Gomorrah set in a familiarly English landscape. The actual poem consists of a lively dialogue between the Dreamer and an unidentified Old Man, and both systematically discuss the underlying sins that have led to the annihilation of the biblical cities, all the while making pointed remarks about the situation in contemporary England.

In addition to showcasing Hogarde's theological and rhetorical knowledge, *A Mirroure of Myserie* is indebted to late medieval and early Tudor literature. In the manner of the *Piers Plowman* tradition Hogarde's persona falls into a dream atop a hill and surveys the moral landscape of England, a scene portrayed in the single illustration contained in HM 121 on fol. 6r. Joseph

---

[7] Andy Wood, *The 1549 Rebellions and the Making of Early Modern England* (Cambridge: Cambridge University Press, 2007), 156.

[8] Ibid., 42.

Martin also notes similarities in Hogarde's poem with the 'Commonwealth men' of the 1549 risings and with Robert Crowley's pamphlets.[9]

The manuscript, HM 121, measures 135 × 170 mm / 5.3 × 6.7 inches and consists of 26 parchment folios with three flyleaves each at the start and end of the volume. *A Mirroure of Myserie* is the sole text in this volume.[10] For a detailed description of the manuscript and its provenance, consult the entry for HM 121 in the *Digital Scriptorium*: http://ds.lib.berkeley.edu/HM00121_43

Editorial note

I have modernised *I/J*, *i/j*, and *u/v*. Roman numerals have been replaced with Arabic numbers, suspensions and contractions have been expanded, capitalisation has been adjusted, and punctuation has been modernised.

All references to *Piers Plowman* (henceforth PP) are to A.V.C. Schmidt, P*iers Plowman: A Parallel-Text Edition of A, B, C and Z Versions* (Kalamazoo: Medieval Institute Publications, 2008); all references to the Bible are to the Douay-Rheims text.

---

9 Martin, *Religious Radicals in Tudor England*, 104.
10 For HM 121 as a gift for Mary, see Richard McCabe, *'Ungainefull Arte': Poetry, Patronage, and Print in the Early Modern Era* (Oxford: Oxford University Press, 2016), 89–90.

Fig. 1. San Marino, CA, Huntington Library, MS HM 121, fol. 6r. (detail)

TEXT

[fol. 1r]
A mirroure of myserie, newly compiled and sett forthe by Myles Huggarde, servaunte to the quenes[1] moste excellente majestie. Anno Domini 1557

[fol. 2r]
To the moste excellente and vertuouse ladie and oure moste graciouse sovereigne, Mary by the grace of God Quene of Englande, Spayne,[2] Fraunce bothe[3] Cicilies, Jerusalem, and Irelande, Defendoure of the Faith, Archeduchesse of Austrie, Duchesse of Millayne, Burgundie, and Brabant, Countesse of haspurge, Flaunders, and Tyroll. Youre majesties moste faithfulle loving ande obediente servaunte Myles Huggarde wisheth all grace, longe[4] peace, and quyett reigne frome God the Father, the Sonne, and the Holye Ghoste.

---

1 *quenes*: Mary I Tudor (1516–58), Queen of England from 1553 until 1558.

2 *Spayne ... Tyroll*: except for the claim to France, Mary acquired her continental titles through her marriage to Philip II of Spain in 1554 (Judith M. Richards, 'Mary Tudor as "Sole Quene"?: Gendering Tudor Monarchy', *The Historical Journal* 40, no. 4 [1997]: 913).

3 *bothe Cicilies*: a common name for the Kingdom of the Two Sicilies, comprising the kingdoms of Sicily and of Naples.

4 The MS has 'u' for 'n' in 'longe'.

As farre as a guyfte[1] maie goode will expresse,
Geven of the gyver after his degree[2]
(By whiche guyfte so geven) yitt I muste confesse
Thinwarde harte therbie well knowne can not be,
5 For dissemblers maie gyve greate guyfte we se.
Therfore as a guyfte maye showe the harte I saie
Moste hartilie I showe my goode will this waye.

[fol. 2v] Towardes youre maiestie, whom I moste humblie
Beseche to pardon my rudenesse[3] herin:
10 Sithe[4] this simple guifte, compiled thus groslie[5]
As a token that the newe[6] yeare doth begyn,
I presente to youre grace, whome God graunte to wynne
His favoure that this yeare and many mo
Youre highnes may reigne and vanquyshe all woo.

15 And moste graciouse Quene it maie seme that I
For lacke of other thing, whiche more mete[7] were
To presente youre grace, then thus baselie[8]
With suche a rude booke every yeare
To troble youre highness, and yitt doth apere
20 I am always harpynge upon one stringe,
As thoughe my penne coulde none other frute bringe.

Whiche in dede can little otherwise do
Both for lacke of witt and eke[9] experience,
Butt whan other matters I wolde applie to
25 Againste God by synne, I se suche offence

---

1 *guyfte*: gift.
2 *degree*: social rank.
3 *rudenesse*: ignorance.
4 *Sithe*: since.
5 *groslie*: clumsily.
6 *newe ... begyn*: 1557, some time after 25 March, the beginning of the year.
7 *mete*: fitting.
8 *baselie*: humbly.
9 *eke*: also.

I can not but therin saie my conscience,
Which stirreth me to sett[1] other thing a parte,
And thus againste synne to open my harte.

[fol. 3r.] Then weyinge with my selfe the greate punysh-
     mente
30   Whiche God did exhibit in every age
On those that by synne did hym discontente,
To thende that same synne in them shoulde asswage.
Then thinkynge of synne, the horrible rage
In Sodom[2] and Gomhorre – alas, my hert did rewe! –
35   Sith some of theire synnes I sawe we did ensewe.[3]

Whiche movith me nowe to marvaile muche lesse
At the plages of God, whiche longe felte have we
(And yitt not so moche as oure synfulnesse
Hath deserved) – this plainly we may se.
40   Yitt we persiste still in oure iniquitie
Before oure lorde God as he[4] nothinge sawe
Of Hym and his plages: we are not in awe!

For the whiche cause, I saie, this little booke
I have compiled, to thende we maie all
45   As in a myrroure on those cities looke,
How horriblie there for theire synnes did fall,
And that we therbie to oure myndes may call
Yf we by oure synnes will still offende God.
As[5] theie did not so, we shall not escape His rodde.

50   [fol. 3v.] Therfore to amende God graunte us His grace
And preserve youre highness in longe felicitie,

---

1   *sett … parte*: dismiss.
2   *Sodom … Gomhorre*: Sodom and Gomorrah, two biblical cities destroyed by God as punishments for the sins of their inhabitants (Genesis 18–19).
3   *ensewe*: imitate.
4   *he*: he who.
5   *As … so*: As those who did not reflect on their sins.

All youre maiesties foose[1] therbie to deface,[2]
Debarringe falshede, and place equitie
Thatt oure common welth renewed may be.
55 Throughe[3] Covetousenes brought in greate decaie,
For thamendement[4] whereof all goode men doth praye.

Youre highness' pore humble servaunte Myles Huggard.

[fol. 4r.] The prologe

Where welth dothe want, and woo increase
Man may that wante bewaile,
For wantynge welthe all joyes doth cease,
And woo doth there prevaile.

5 This wante of welthe in men private
Dothe eche in hym selfe showe
Of that contrie the woofull state
Wheare welth it doth not knowe.

Whan this wante waxeth[5] generall,
10 As here we have it knowe,
Then common welthe it dothe apall[6]
And is[7] quyte over throwue.

[fol. 4v.] The cause wherof consideringe
To be for synne onlie.
15 I thought ensample here to brynge
That we frome synne shoulde flye.

---

1   *foose*: foes.
2   *deface*: destroy.
3   *Throughe ... decaie*: Through greed [our commonwealth has been] brought in great decay.
4   *thamendement*: correction.
5   *waxeth generall*: becomes common.
6   *apall*: tire, weaken.
7   *is*: the verb refers to 'common welthe'.

And the rather because I see
Like[1] synnes emongest us raigne.
As the prophett[2] notith to bee
20   Cause of those peoples payne,

Whiche in Sodom and Gomhorre were,
Onlie one[3] synne, excepte[4]
Whiche for the filthynes oughte here
In silence to be kepte.

25   [fol. 5r.] Yitt oughte no man here for to thinke
That synne the cause alone
Thatt all thies greate Cities did sinke
And consumed eche one.

The sortes of synnes, is playne noted
30   By good Ezecheell,[5]
Wherwith theire soules was foule spotted,
Whiche herafter I tell

Requirynge you, goode reders, all
to accepte my good will.
35   And where faltes be mende them I shall,
Youre pleasures to fulfill.

[fol. 5v.] Synne to reprove I do delite,
Thoughe I moste synfull be.

---

[1] *Like*: similar.

[2] *prophett*: Ezekiel 16:49–50. Alternatively, this may also refer to Isaiah, who stresses the causal link between sin and the destruction of Sodom and Gomorrah most explicitly among the prophets of the Old Testament (Isaiah 1:9–10; 3:9, and 13:19–22).

[3] *one synne*: homosexuality (Genesis 19:4–5).

[4] *except*: excepting.

[5] Ezekiel 16:49–50: 'Behold this was the iniquity of Sodom thy sister, pride, fulness of bread, and abundance, and the idleness of her, and of her daughters: and they did not put forth their hand to the needy, and to the poor'.

If I the truthe in thinges do write,
40　I truste none will blame me.

　　Wisshinge[1] oure synfulness to cease
　　Yf we will welthe possesse,
　　For God oure plages will not release
　　Yf still we so transgresse.

45　Who[2] graunte us grace; we shortlie maie
　　Applie oure willes to His.
　　Then shall we at oure endynge daie
　　Enjoy eternall blysse!

[The poem] [+illustration, *fig.* 1]

[fol. 6r.] Beinge in studie of the worldes estate[3]
weyinge the workes of every wyghte,[4]
Alas, my corage it did clene abate[5]
Frome all Joyfulnes to Joy[6] in of righte.
5　Penury[7] his Pavilion had pighte[8]
Heare forto remayne, wherbie I did see
Pore[9] and riche punshed in theire degree.

All menne whiche are of noble progeny
Theire estate this day right well may bewayle,
10　Considerynge, as thaie maye if they vew thorowly,

1　*Wisshinge ... possesse*: we desire to lead a less sinful life if we have acquired material wealth.
2　*Who*: He who (i.e., God).
3　*estate*: condition.
4　*wyghte*: person.
5　*abate*: lessen, withdraw.
6　*Joy ... righte*: unclear. Perhaps deserved joy or redemption as opposed to carefree joy.
7　*Penury ... pighte*: PP, A. 2.41: 'Was piȝt vp a pauyloun proud for þe nones'.
8　*pighte*: pitched.
9　*Pore ... riche*: this phrase appears frequently in PP, starting with A and B Prol. 18.

Howe farre frome theire fathers theyre fame doth fayle
Touching howse[1] kepynge, for pore folkes availe[2]
A Plage it may be, as trewly it is,
to the hartes of suche as dothe thinke of this.

15 [fol. 6v.] Pore menne eke are plaged by penurye
Receyvinge of some riche menne but smalle relefe.
For lacke of foode, thaie saie, many dothe die
Of hunger was never felte the like grefe.
Butt of all this woo what shoulde be causee cheefe?
20 This entringe my heade I was at a staye.[3]
So many I sawe, I wiste not whatt to saye.

The nombre was suche here dayly sene
Thatt I, studyinge the right cause to conceyve,
Was forced, as I many tymes have bene,
The foly of fancy for to deceyve,
25 To walke abrode suche pleasure to receyve
As tyme dothe mynyster in geminy,[4]
when flore[5] the erthe dothe freshly beautyfie.

The pleasure wherof so ravished my witte
That layinge[6] me downe in a slepe I fell.
30 Morpheus,[7] the god of dreames, spyinge[8] it,

---

1 *howse kepynge*: owning property or running an estate.
2 *availe*: help, support.
3 *staye*: standstill.
4 *geminy*: when the sun is in the sign of Gemini, between the end of spring and late summer (Rachel Fletcher, 'The Geometry of the Zodiac', *Nexus Network Journal* [2009]: 114).
5 *flore*: flowers.
6 *layinge ... fell*: the dreaming narrator *PP* also falls asleep in late spring in similar circumstances: *PP* A and B Prol. 11; C Prol. 8.
7 *Morpheus*: the Greek god of sleep. Morpheus sleep-inducing powers are summoned in a number of medieval dream poems, including Geoffrey Chaucer's *Book of the Duchess*.
8 *spyinge*: espying.

Placed[1] hym in fancy[2] wheare ofte dothe dwell,
And theare all my studie he perceyvinge well
Did take me by the hand, and as me thoughte,
He saide straunge thinges to my sighte shoulde be broughte.

35 [fol. 7r.] Then forthe he led me frome thence as I was.
In whatt sorte[3] I wente it paste frome my mynde,
Butt therin, me thoughte, he tooke smalle solace.[4]
Wee flewe,[5] to my semynge, more swifte than the mynde.
I wondered whether he had me assynde[6]
40 For over seas and mowntaynes we toke oure flighte.
Then in a straunge place wee at lengthe did alighte,

Whiche was uppon an hill, pleasaunte and hie,
Wheare, as he lefte me standynge alone,
Then leynge my selfe theare, 'Oh, Lorde!', thought I,
45 'Heare am I comfortles. All my joyes are gone'.
And as I stoode thus, makynge this mone,[7]
Sodenlie an olde manne to me did apert,[8]
who, whan he spied me, began to drawe nere.

---

1   *Placed ... broughte*: this passage and subsequent stanzas are modelled on Kynde granting the dreaming Will a vista of Creation from Mount Middle Earth in *PP* B.320–67. In the C text the mountain of Middle Earth becomes the 'myrour of Mydelerthe' (132); the equivalent passage in C is in 13.131–78.
2   *fancy*: imagination.
3   *sorte*: manner.
4   *solace*: delight.
5   *flewe*: although this passage draws on *PP* B.11 and Kynde lifting Will onto the top of Mount Middle Earth, the noetic flight of the narrator here echoes a similar passage in Chaucer's *House of Fame*, where an oversized eagle carries the dreaming Geoffrey, granting him a similarly revealing view of Creation (Larry D. Benson, *The Riverside Chaucer* [Oxford: Oxford University Press, 1987], ll. 896–909).
6   *assynde*: ascent.
7   *mone*: complaint.
8   *apert*: appear.

Streighte he asked me whatt I did there make
50 And whi I loked so sorowfullie.
'Alas', quod[1] I, 'some pitie on me take
For I can not tell how I came nor whie.
I thinke in this place sure I shall die'
'Nay, for that be thawe[2] not sory', quod he.
55 'Feare thowe nothinge; thie warraunte[3] I will be'.

[fol. 7v.] 'Thowe haste no cause[4] here, thou seist, to be ladde,[5]
Sythe all thinges plentie dothe here brede and growe
That for thie bodie is mete[6] to be hadde –
Mylke and hony dothe this land overflowe.
60 The lyke, I dare saie, thow diddest never knowe'.
'What,[7] for thatt', quod I, 'I had rather bee
In my pore Cottage in myne owne contrie'.

'I beleve the', quod he, 'so saide the Jewes,
To whome this[8] contrie was longe promysed.
65 Havynge in wildernes, as scripture[9] shewes,
Meate[10] that frome above to them descended,
And theire[11] clothes also no[12] whitte peryshed,
Thus cled and fed, theye were, for 40 yeares spare,
Yitt to be contente thaye had not the grace'.

---

1 *quod*: said.
2 *thawe*: thou, second person singular pronoun.
3 *warraunte*: protector.
4 *cause*: motive, reason.
5 *ladde*: led, brought.
6 *mete*: meet, fitting, in the sense of 'nourishing'.
7 *What*: well.
8 *this contrie*: Israel.
9 *scripture ... spare*: Exodus 16:1–36.
10 *Meate*: food, here the biblical manna given to the Israelites following their Exodus from Egypt.
11 *theire ... peryshed*: Deuteronomy 29:5.
12 *no whitte*: not in the least.

70 Then at this talke to muse muche I beganne
   And wiste nott whatt I shoulde therto saye.
   'Is this', quod I, 'the lande of Canaan?'[1]
   'Yea, that it is', quod he, 'well perceyve thou maye'.
   'And I was in Englande', quod I, 'once to daye'.
75 'Whatt then', quod he, 'thou waste hither broughte
   By that whiche was as swifte as thy thoughte?'

[fol. 8r.] 'That maie be so', quod I, 'for trulie I
   Can not Imagyn thexcedinge swyftnesse
   That I in the aire did hitherwarde flie,
80 And nowe am lefte here in greate distresse
   For what he mente therbie he did not expresse'.
   'What he mente, it dothe not skill',[2] quod he.
   'Sithe thou arte lette in this pleasaunte contree

   Wherin to rest, it thow causte be contente.
85 More worldlie welth no wight can here attayne.
   [*margin*: Gene: 12] Oure[3] father Abraham[4] hither was sente,
   This[5] land to enjoye, the scripture is playne.
   And his seede also for ever to remayne'.
   'Yitt', quod I, 'theie fell into captivitie
90 And loste that land. How doth this agree?'

   'It semith', quod he, 'as I tolde the before,
   That as the Jewes of theire welth were wery
   And loste this lande therfore for evermore,

---

1 *Canaan*: the Israelites reached Canaan after forty years of wandering (Exodus 16:35).
2 *skill*: matter (verb).
3 *oure … playne*: Genesis 12.1–8.
4 *Abraham*: the Old Testament patriarch.
5 *This land*: Canaan.

[margin: Num: 14] Excepte[1] Josua[2] and Caleb onelie
95 [margin: Deut: 1] Nott one came in it of all that company[3]
Whose unfaithfulnes was onlie the lett.[4]
I thinke thowe and they are all even[5] well mett'.

[fol. 8v.] 'For thow enjoying this lande dost doubtes caste,
As thow of thie welth forced,[6] nothinge
100 Thowe regardest more. Thie worldie state paste,
Then here to enjoye a pleasaunte lyvynge.
Therfore leave of the[7] thie folyshe reasonynge,
Lest fro this place thow be quite banyshed
And also frome the places[8] by this figured'.

105 'Of what is it', quod I, 'a figure[9] then?'
'Of heaven', quod he, 'as all lerned men saie'.
'Then me thinke', quod I, 'they spake butt like men
Fo it can figure heaven aptlie no waye,
Which, as I take it, prove thus I maye:
110 [margin: Num: 20] Moyses[10] nor Aron entred not this land,
Thoughe in goddes favoure highly they did stande'.

'Now, if this lande muste heaven signyfye,
How dothe the truthe – the figure – aunswere[11] here?
Moyses never entred it. Personallie

---

1 *Excepte ... company*: of the twelve spies sent by Moses to examine Canaan only Joshua and Caleb were allowed to enter the Promised Land (Numbers 13–14).
2 *Josua ... Caleb*: two tribal leaders sent by Moses to Canaan (Numbers 13).
3 *company*: the Israelites.
4 *lett*: hindrance, impediment.
5 *even ... mett*: equal (to one another).
6 *forced*: compelled, overpowered in the sense of having lost his wealth through force.
7 *the*: then.
8 *places ... figured*: places represented by this place, i.e., figuratively.
9 *figure*: allegory, metaphor.
10 *Moyses ... stande*: Numbers 20. The Old Testament prophets and brothers Moses and Aaron.
11 *aunswere*: confirm.

115 Therfore, I saye to me it doth appeare
　　The figure the truth herin will not bere
　　For I beleve Moyses is in heaven sure
　　Whiche can no be aunsweringe the figure.'

[fol. 9r.] 'Nere[1] thow maiest knowe thyne ignoraunce' quod he.
120 'All figures whiche did Christe prefigurate
　　Did not in all poyntes poyntinglie[2] agree,
　　As no poynte therin should be vacuate.[3]
　　Christe is calde a lyon butt after what rate?[4]
　　[*margin*: Apoc: 5.] Not[5] as a lyon is a beaste ravynouse
125 Butt as a lyon is a beaste victoriouse!'

'So thoughe Moises and Aron, entred not here
　　To enjoy this lande, as they did purpose.
　　The cause in scripture doth playnlie apere:
　　For mystrustinge God this lande they did lose,
130 Yitt did he nott use[6] them, as[7] he did his fole,
　　[*margin*: Deutro: 32.] But of his frutefull lande he gave them sighte.
　　The figure in parte is here aunswered righte.'

'For this was to them (sithe God so wolde it)
　　Nott onlie a cause theire synnes to lamente,
135 Butt praised God – not grudgyng any whitt –
　　That theire ofsprynge shoulde there be residentm
　　So it followes nott, thoughe theie were nott here present,
　　Thatt therfore in heaven they cannott now be
　　Because to the figure it dothe not hole agree.'

1　*Nere*: soon.
2　*poyntinglie*: exactly.
3　*vacuate*: empty, as in 'ignored'.
4　*rate*: proportion or aspect of a whole.
5　*Not … victoriouse*: Apocalypse 5:5.
6　*use*: treat.
7　*as … fole*: Deuteronomy 32:1–43.

140 [fol. 9v.] 'Did the sighte', quod I, 'as moche truth implie
Touching the aunsweringe of the figure
As thoughe the pleasure they had bodilye
Enjoyed in this lande? I thinke not so, sure.
For as hunger to eate doth man allure,
145 Then to quenche the same what helpis sight of meate[1]
To the hungrie man if he none therof eate?'

'So God to the Jewes did promyse this lande
Who, as ye saie, for theire unfaithfulnesse
And grudginge at God, as I understande,
150 Perished in the waie and did nott possesse.
Yea, Moises and Aron did lykewise transgresse,
Entringe no further butt[2] onlie to the sighte
Were[3] nott theire pleasures all lyke matched righte'.

'And yitt if I shoulde saie my conscience,
155 To Moyses and Aron the sighte was more payne,
Havinge there no bodily residence
Where theie sawe so greate pleasures remeyne,
Then it was to those whom God did disdayne,
Nott suffering them neither to enter nor see.
160 This to me doth apere moste trewe to bee'.

[fol. 10r.] 'Remembrest thow not', quod he, 'that I erste[4] saide?
The sighte of this land such penaunce in them wroughte
Sith by theire follie frome it theie were staied.[5]
Seynge to what pleasure they shoulde here have bene broughte
165 That God (who ever for manes health hath wrougthe)

---

1 *meate*: food in general.
2 *butt ... sighte*: but were only granted a glimpse.
3 *Were ... righte*: where their identical delight (at seeing the land of Canaan) dit not match their (lack of) entitlement.
4 *erste*: earlier.
5 *staied*: prevented, excluded.

For that theire pennaunce by that sighte moved
Showeth them of God to be dearlie loved'.

'Furthermore, where God suffred them to see
This frutefull lande and the pleasures therin
170 To the truth dothe very aptlie agree
Sithe the greatest joye that man in heaven can wynne
[*margin*: Psalm: 63.[1]] Is the sighte[2] of God, which heare to begynne
[*margin*: Ioh: 17.] To expresse doth[3] passe all mortall mennes witt.
Then the figure beinge sight the truth answers it'.

175 'This begyns', quod I, 'to come somwhatt nere
To resolve the doubtes wherein I late was.
Then', quod I,[4] 'sithe that doth to the apere,
I will showe the a sighte or[5] thowe hence passe –
Whiche to show the doth greve my harte, alas'.
180 'Thow toldest me', quod I, 'here was all pleasure!
'Can pleasure, I pray the, have sorrowe in[6] ure?'

[fol. 10v.] 'Yea', quod he, 'so moste conveniente
For the Catholicke Churche on erth mylytante[7]
Figureth heaven where Joy is ever permanent,
185 And therfore we call it the Church triumphaunte'.
'Yit the Churche on erthe, I thinke, thou wilte graunte

---

1 63: not 63 but 61:8.
2 *sighte ... God*: Psalm 61:8.
3 *doth ... witt*: probably either John 17:25 or John 1:18.
4 *I*: a mistake for 'he'.
5 *or*: before.
6 *in ure*: bring about, effect.
7 *mylytante*: the Church Militant, as opposed to the Church Triumphant, is the community of the Christians on Earth, locked in constant struggle with secular powers. The Church Militant is a central concern of PP and many works written in the *Piers Plowman* tradition.

Thoughe it figure heaven, yitt the name doth expresse
That it reignethe not here ver[1] in quietnesse'.

'And wheare thow thinkest it an inconvenience[2]
190 That I shoulde show the here eny carefull[3] sighte
Because this place in pleasure hath preheminence,[4]
Me thinke reason in this should give the sighte
Because in the Scripture[5] thou haste a rule righte
That God, his aungells, and his sainctes also
195 Seith "frome hence mens wickednes and how their lyves doth go"'.

'So, I saie, frome hence a sighte thou shalte see
Whiche will move the inwardlie to lamente
How God hathe punyshed menns iniquitie,
Whiche maie move the worlde suche vice to repente'.
200 With that to the edge of an hie[6] hill we wente,
Where he poynted me a contrie to vewe,
At the sighte whereof I founde his wordes trewe.

[fol. 11r.] For there I sawe a contrie quite overflowne
With filthie water, moste foule and stynkinge.
205 'Yonder', quod he, 'was welthie cities knowne'.
Whiche vewing at that word to my thinkinge
I saw the toppes of turrette still sinkinge.
'Alas', quod I, 'whatt contrie was this
That sonke into therthe so horriblie is?'

---

1 *ver*: ever.
2 *inconvenience*: unnatural occurence.
3 *carefull*: sorrowful, distressing.
4 *preheminence*: preeminence, in the sense of being characterised by something.
5 *Scripture … go*: this does not appear to be a reference to any particular passage in the Bible, though it may invoke the expulsion of Adam and Eve from Paradise in Genesis 3.
6 *hie hill*: the elevation and vista presented to the narrator recalls Mount Middle Ealth in *PP* B.320–67.

210 'Yonder stode the welthie Cities', quod hee
    'Of Sodom and Gomhor, and other mo,
    Whose wicked workes were of such iniquitee
    That in the nose of God theire sinnes did stinke so
    [*margin*: Gen: 19.] That He[1] willed Loth with all his stock thence to go,
215 And that to looke backe they shoulde in no wise,
    Butt yitt did Lothes wife, Goddes preceptes dispise'.

'For that whiche she was turned into a salte stone
Because that as salte doth make meate saverye,
She shoulde emonge others ensample be one
220 That before nor since was not seene with eye,
To thende that the worlde shoulde therbie
To Goddes preceptes evermore to obeie
And nott againste His will to worke theire owne waie'.

[fol. 11v.] 'Alas', quod I, 'what synnes did they commytt
225 That God so greate vengeaunce on them did take?'
'Forsoth,'[2] quod he, 'the prophett[3] showith it:
Of foure synnes greate rehersall he doth make
Whiche caused Goddes grace in them so to slake
That there fell to the fifte synne now to name
230 To the at this tyme I will not for shame'.

'Yitt tell me', quod I, 'whiche those foure synnes were
Uppon the whiche the fifte synne did ensewe?'
[*margin*: Ezeche: 16.] 'That', quod he, 'in[4] Ezecheell doth apere:
[*margin*: Pride.] Pride was the firste synne, whiche theie sore did rewe´.
235 'Pride', quod I, 'God forbid – it shoulde be trew!'

---

1   *He ... stone*: Genesis 19:15–26.
2   *Forsoth*: truly.
3   *prophett*: Ezekiel.
4   *in Ezecheell*: Ezekiel 16:49.

'Truth', quod he, 'it is; the Prophett can not lye'.
'Then God have mercie uppon us!', quod I.

'For in Englande, sithe I firste remember, maie
More pride nor the like pride was never seene.
240 Ambicion hath broughte a nombre to decaie,
As by experience tried[1] this hathe bene.
God and theire prince they have forgott clene.
Pride theire wicked hartes doth so elevate
Thatt proudlie theie wolde clyme above theire estate'.

245 [fol. 12r.] [*margin*: The pride vaynegloriouse of heretikes, pryde of lerning, Connynge, Beautie, Auctorytie, and also of manye other thinges.]
'Pryde besides this manie braunches hathe,
The whiche upon vaineglory do depende,
As namelie those whiche repugnith the faith.
So many wayes that if I tyme shoulde spende
To showe them all, I should not make an ende,
250 I thinke, all this daie, and therfore will I
Say no more leste I shoulde make yow wery'.

[*margin*: Pride in apparell.] 'Yitt maie I not slippe[2] the greate excesse
The whiche in England doth remaine at this daie
In vayne apparell, wherbie theie transgresse
255 Both God and mannes lawes. And yitt, I dare saie,
[*margin*: Paynfull pryde] Yf[3] payne by pride forced coulde theire pride staie,
Some in theire purses shoulde nott be so bare
whiche nowe to other uses hath small to spare'.

---

1 *tried*: confirmed, proved.
2 *slippe*: omit.
3 *Yf … spare*: If suffering as a consequence of their pride could force them to contain their pride, then some of them wouldn't have purses so empty that they leave them with only little to spend on other causes.

'That this is a plage and a payne grevouse
260　Where the purse is emptie, recorde I. Take[1]
Of those whose apparell is righte gorgiouse
(Thoughe yitt to the worlde a faire fate theie make),
Butt and it credit towarde such men did slake.
Theire apparell by theire purses wolde appere
265　For after theire paymente theire clothes theie should were.'

[fol. 12v.] 'And then, I doubte not, butt as tholde proverbe saith:
"A[2] purse that is withoute money, saie thaye,
Is like a bodie the whiche no soule hath".
I doubte nottt it credit did faile them, I saye.
270　Theire pursis emptie, theire joyes wolde delaie.
Theie wolde to the worlde as jocunde apere
As if theire soules in an other worlde were'.

'This pride dothe pynche them with privye[3] payne,
Thoughe the world they will not be aknowne.[4]
275　The mercer and draper with[5] other knowith playne
To whome faire wordes so many swete blastes hath blowne
On those which are not proude therof one whitt
Butt raither repentith theire hastie creditt'.[6]

1　*Take ... were*: Only take away the garments from those whose clothes are luxurious, and though to the world their clothers project material success, the good will extended to such people will diminish.

2　*A ... hath*: this proverb is usually associated with Martin Luther's argument for the importance of spoken words in the celebration of the sacraments: 'Without them, the sacraments are dead and empty, like a body without a soul, a cask without wine, a purse without money' (Robert C. Croken, *Luther's First Front: The Eucharist as Sacrifice* [Ottawa: University of Ottawa Press, 1990], 19).

3　*privye*: secret.

4　*aknowne*: laid open, revealed (to the world).

5　*with other*: and others.

6　*creditt*: reputation, good standing.

'Yitt is pride paynfull in some besides this
280 In thinges worne for pride and unprofitable.
I will not tell in whome this pride proved is,
Butt sure it is thought muche discommendable,[1]
And to the wearers nothinge profitable.
Butt I thinke sure if it were not for pride
285 The payne therof wolde sone saie[2] suche thinges aside'.

[fol. 13r.] 'This is to me a darke[3] sayinge', quod he.
'What doest thow meane? This kynde of pride to name
Which thou notist unprofitable to be
And discomendable to open[4] this same?'
290 'I dare not', quod I, 'lest some will me blame'.
'Tushe!',[5] quod he, 'what nedist thow to feare
Sith no man butt I thie councell doth heare?'

'Then', quod I, 'under benedicite,[6]
Trewlie, by womens vardingales[7] I meane'.
295 'What maner of garment is that?', quod he.
'The name I have not herde, nor the garmente seene'.
'No mervaile, quod I, 'for it hathe not bene
Anonge them longe usid. Yitt herde I whan
Some wearers curste those that them first[8] began'.

300 'Then belike',[9] quod he 'thaie are to[10] straite layste?'
'Nott a whitt', quod I, 'where vardingales are worne.

---

1 *discommendable*: to be disapproved of.
2 *saie ... aside*: see such things be set aside.
3 *dark*: unclear.
4 *open ... same*: reveal this very type of pride.
5 *Tushe!*: disparaging exclamation, 'nonsense!'.
6 *benedicite*: 'good gracious!'.
7 *vardingales*: farthingales, frameworks of hoops worked into some kind of cloth, formerly used for extending the skirts of women's dresses (OED).
8 *first began*: Mary I is usually credited with having been one of the first to introduce this style to England.
9 *belike*: probably.
10 *to ... layste*: laced too tightly.

For the pride of them is beneth the wayste:
All theire clothes therwith a grete bredth is borne,
Sett out with hopes,[1] almost herde[2] as horne'.
305 'Perhappes', quod he, 'it is to gether wynde?'
'In winter', quod I, 'no suche cause theie fynde'.

[fol. 13v.] 'In winter', quod he, 'theie were them not I trowe!'
'That theie do', quod I, 'and is it not a payne
To weare suche garmente, in colde froste and snowe?'
'Bye[3] ladie', quod he, 'that I beleve playne!'
310 'Yitt do they', quod I, 'more than this susteyne,
For on horsbacke or stoole theie sitt not at ease,
Yitt for pride they seme not it shoulde them displease'.

'Trulie I have knowene whan the tyme hathe bene
That honest women wolde have beene ashamed
315 Theire clothes borne up so hie to be sene.
Butt belike theie thinke the worlde is tamed,
And with suche sightes will not be enflamed.
Ys not this thinke,[4] ye, discomendable?'
'Yea, god graunte', quod he, 'it be not as damnable'.

320 'I will saie no more', quod I, 'for feare of offence.
Butt unprofitable[5] theie[6] knowe that theie[7] be
Besides the price, whiche is a vayne expence
And displeasith God muche, I do feare me'.
'Doubteles theie shall aunswere for it', quod he,

---

[1] *hopes*: hoops.
[2] *herde ... horne*: farthingale hoops were typically made of whalebone.
[3] *Bye ladie*: by Our Lady.
[4] *thinke*: thing.
[5] *unprofitable*: harmful.
[6] *theie*: people.
[7] *theie*: farthingales.

325 And for all superfluouse things in like sorte,
    As Elai[1] the prophet doth to us reporte:

> [fol. 14r.] [*margin*: Elai: 3.] "The doughters of Syon are so proude", saith he,
> "With stretched oute neckes and wanton eies vayne
> Trippinge with theire feete as nice[2] as may be.
> 330 Therfore shall God shave theire heades playne
> And theire gorgiouse raymente[3] from them restrayne,[4]
> As spanges,[5] cheynes, collers, brooches, and bracelette,
> wide embrothered rayment, ringe, and partelette".[6]

'Thies dothe he name with many things mo,
335 Wherewith by pride thies women did offende.
    The whiche to punyshe God did threaten sore,[7]
    Whiche threates to Christen women eke doth extende,
    And shall be punyshed if theie not amende,
    Whose excesssyve pride is more at this daie
340 Then it was in Jury'.[8] 'Truth', quod I, 'no[9] naye'.

'Alas', quod I, 'yitt it grevith my harte
    To heare that this contrie for synne did sinke,
    And namelie that pride was cause therof a parte.
    Suche pryde emonge them was not more, I thinke,
345 Then is nowe in Englande, at whiche to wynke[10]

---

1   *Elai ... partelette*: Isaiah 3:16–23.
2   *nice*: foolishly.
3   *raymente*: adornment.
4   *restrayne*: withdraw.
5   *spanges*: spangles, glittering ornaments.
6   *partelette*: an item of clothing worn over the neck and upper part of the chest (OED).
7   *sore*: grievously.
8   *Jury*: Judea; the land of the Israelites.
9   *no naye*: indeed.
10   *wynke*: close his eyes, make an exception.

God doth not showe, for his plage dothe us threate,
That[1] his displeasure againste us is greate'.

[fol. 14v.] 'Yt muste nedes be so', quod he, 'where pride doth reigne.
For pride drove Lucyfere[2] frome Heaven to helle.
350 By pride oure firste[3] parente did Goddes hestes[4] disdayne,
For whiche into[5] great myserie they felle.
Nabuchodonozor[6] wolde God in heaven excelle,
For whiche pride God make hym 7 yeares a beaste.
Thus to punyshe Pride God yitt never ceaste'.

355 [*margin*: the seconde synne of the Sodomytes.] 'Now the sconde synne ensuynge this pride
Was fulness[7] of meate, with so greate excesse
Thatt frome all honestie theie were as farre wide
As those whiche never had herde godlynesse'.
'Did fulnes of meate', quod I, 'as you expresse,
Oure Lord God here so grevouslie offende?'
360 'Thou maiste[8] perceive that', quod he, 'by theire ende'.

Alas, with that worde my herte was gone quyte.
'Then', quod I, 'wo maie we be in Englande
For in excesse of meate we so muche delite
That oute of feare of God and man we stande
365 To feede the carcase we[9] so take in hande
That the pamperinge therof we do more regarde

---

1 *That*: so that.
2 *Lucyfere*: the rebel angel who led a revolt against God (Isaiah 14:12).
3 *firste parente*: Adam and Eve.
4 *hestes*: behests, orders.
5 *into ... felle*: Genesis 3.
6 *Nabuchodonozor*: Nebuchadnezzar II, king of Babylon in the sixth century BCE. In Daniel 4 Nebuchadnezzar's madness leads him to live seven feral years in the wilderness.
7 *fulness ... meate*: excess of food, gluttony.
8 *maiste ... perceive*: can see.
9 *we*: that we.

Then by punyshing it to have Goddes rewarde'.

[fol. 15r.] 'Do[1] they beleve eny rewarde', quod he, 'trowist thow,
At Goddes hand to be had for fastinge frome meate?'
370 'I thinke not', quod I, 'for then theie wolde allowe
That[2] kynde of fast to be a vertu greate
Sith of the vile flesh it doth kille the heate
Beinge Joyned with praier, as it shoulde be'.
'That is not unlike to be trwe', quod he.

375 [*margin*: Deut:[3] 34. / 3 Regu:[4] 21. / 1 Esdr:[5] 8.&2. / Esdr: 1. / Iudith:[6] 4. / Hest:[7] 4. / Luc:[8] 14. / Math:[9] 6.] 'Yitt if theie rede Scripture advisedlie,
Settinge theire carnall[10] affeccions aparte,
Theie shall fynde that those which God favoured hie
By thoutwarde fastinge did showe thinwarde herte'.
'To be penytente butt', quod I, 'overthwarte[11]
380 Frome that kynde of pennaunce the worlde is gone.
Of[12] all partes therof theie thinke fastinge none'.

---

1 *Do ... meate?*: 'Do you think', he said, 'that they believe that any reward can be obtained from God by abstaining from food?'
2 *That ... praier*: 'In combination with prayer this kind of fasting can neutralise the hot humour [underlying the desire to crave more food] of the corrupted body'.
3 *Deut 34*: probably a mistake for Deuteronomy 9, where Mostes fasts on Mount Sinai.
4 *3 Regu 21*: 1 Kings 21.
5 *1 Esdr: 8.&2 ... Esdr: 1*: Ezra 8:21–23. 'Esdr: 1' could be mistake, in combination with the preceding digits, for 'Esdr. 8.&21', i.e., Ezra 8:21.
6 *Iudith: 4*: Judith 4:7–11.
7 *Hest: 4*: Esther 4:3 and 16.
8 *Luc: 14*: Luke 14 is not concerned fasting but with humbling oneself and hosting feasts for those in need.
9 *Math: 6*: Matthew 6:16–18.
10 *carnall affections*: carnal pleasures, here delight in food.
11 *overthwarte*: opposite.
12 *Of ... none*: 'They did not regard fasting as being a part of this world'.

'Yitt', quod he, 'oure mother, the Churche Catholike,
Because[1] with vertue all hirs shoulde be fedde,
Forseinge that to fall the fleshe was quicke
385 And unto vertewe wolde hardlie be ledde,
[*margin*: Ioh:[2] 14.] Beinge governde by Gode[3] Spirit, as it[4] is redde,
She poynteth[5] tymes and daies for all hirs to faste,
That[6] God his favoure uppon them may caste'.

[fol. 15v.] 'The whiche all hir children was[7] wonte forto kepe.
390 Knowinge hir preceptes, theie were bounde to obey,
But, alas, my herte for sorrowe dothe wepe
To here that many force not at this day
For the fleshe to caste all vertue awaie,
[*margin*: Tobi:[8] 12] Nott wayinge howe the Churche doth consider
395 How goode it is to faste and praie together'.

'Theie se not that', quod I, 'for theie do not beleve
Thatt the Churche of Christe can man on whit bynde
To obeie to that which doth the fleshe greve.
Bycause by Scripture it is nott allynde'.[9]
400 'Nott so farre', quod he, 'as themselves can fynde.
Ys it not a goode argumente than
Theie can nott fynde it, ergo none other can?'

---

1 *Because*: In order to.
2 *Ioh: 14*: John 14:26.
3 *Gode Spirit*: Holy Spirit.
4 *it ... redde*: can be read.
5 *poynteth*: has appointed, fixed.
6 *That*: So that.
7 *was wonte*: were accustomed.
8 *Tobi*: Tobit 12:8.
9 *allynde*: connected.

'Saincte Mary!', quod I. 'Theie saie sithe theie can rede,
And redinge the Scripture in thinglishe tonge,
405 If it were there, theie coulde finde it in dede
For theire wittes, saie theie, is not therin yonge.'[1]
'Theie be rotten', quod he, 'or theie be halfe[2] spronge,
Which causeth them in Scripture nott to fynde
The thinge thatt soundeth againste theire carnall mynde'.

410 [fol. 16r.] 'Butt sithe neyther redinge nor yitt preachinge
Can restrayne them frome theire excessive fare,
Lett this plage here be to them a teachinge
That God this contrie for synne wold nott spare,
Butt, as you thou seist, did his vengeaunce declare.
415 Doubte not if Englande synne in the like,
He will not faile yit grevouselie to strike!'

'And thinke uppon this what tholde proverbe saithe:
Whan[3] the bellie is full, the bones wolde be at reste.
And to vertewe man no desire hathe,
420 Butt all kynde of vice is then moste preste
Whiche in those wicked people was expreste
For by theire bellie chere of so greate excesse
Theie fell into vice of moste filthynesse'.

'This fedinge the bellie, disdaynynge to faste,
425 The prophett[4] saieth, was one greate procuremente[5]
Thatt God his favoure frome them clene did caste.
Then into filthie synne further theie wente.
Therfore let all men by myne advisemente

---

1 *yonge*: naive, untrained.
2 *halfe spronge*: half-grown.
3 *Whan ... reste*: common proverb, see Roman Dyboski, ed., *Richard Hill's Commonplace Book*, EETS OS 101 (London: Kegan, Paul, Trench, Trübner, 1908), 129.
4 *prophett*: Ezekiel 16:49.
5 *procuremente*: cause.

Call for grace and amende, leste God for synne
430 As he punyshte here to punyshe them begynne'.

[fol. 16v.] 'The thirde thinge whiche caused the launde to fall
Was of worldlie welth greate aboundaunce.
[*margin*: The third cause whiche Sodomites felle was aboundaunce of all worldelye thinges.] Not thankyng God thefore, as gyver of all,
Butt in bellie joie sett all theire pastaunce,[1]
435 Abusinge beastlie theire worldlie substaunce'.
'Alas', quod I, 'did that brynge them in this case?'
'It was a meane',[2] quod he, 'to fall frome Goddes grace'.

'Then', quod I, 'if I mighte be belevid,
Wolde[3] God I were at home in Englande:
440 If with thabuse of riches God be greved,
I wolde theie knewe how the case here doth stande!
This lighte here, I thinke, effectuallie[4] skande,
Wolde frome theire riches to God turne theire love
If grace eny waye frome vice maie them move'.

445 'Doste thou thynke' quod he, 'theie wolde beleve the
Sithe in the Scripture this storie is preude?[5]
And reding it dailie no better theie be,
Butt rather worse and worse God theie offende'.
'God' quod I, 'more grace emonge us all sende
450 And a toward[6] will, the same to obeye
Whiche grace God offeringe we still caste awaye'.

---

1 *pastaunce*: recreation.
2 *meane*: means.
3 *Wolde God*: 'O, that God would'.
4 *effectuallie skande*: thoroughly discerned.
5 *preude*: proved, recorded.
6 *toward*: favourable.

[fol. 17r.] 'So may ye', quod he, 'fall in an evil case.¹
There can be to God no greater offence
Then here wilfullie to refuse his grace.
455 For suche folkes of synn makis no conscience'.
'Of that', quod I, 'we have to muche experience,
For never was there realme to oure lorde more bounde
Then Englande is, and so unthankefull founde!'

'For covytouse² catchinge of worldie riches
460 Is rooted in mens hartes thatt theie do not passe³
By subtilitie and crafte poore men to oppresse.
More gredie, I thinke, than this lande ever was!
Nor did not therbie oure Lorde more trespas
Than England doth now, for whiche dothe appere
465 To punyshe it sore He doth nott forbere'.

'To shhew⁴ the cawtels⁵ of covitouse men
Greate substaunce to gett, I can nott tell all.
In whiche thinge entringe, I can not tell when
To make an ende, and therfore I shall
470 Knytte⁶ it up in a centence butt small:
The covitouse mans eye saithe the wise man
Is never satisfied, gather what he can'.

[fol. 17v.] 'Nor how suche gettith goodes not one whitt theie care'.
'Thatt', quod he, 'the Scripture doth affirme playne:
475 The coytouse man for mony will not spare

---

1 *case*: predicament.
2 *covytouse*: strong desire.
3 *passe*: proceed.
4 *shhew*: reveal.
5 *cawtels*: tricks, strategems.
6 *Knytte … up*: compact, express.

[margin: Miche:[1] 3.] To[2] have the pore mens skynne frome the fleshe flayne
And the fleshe frome the bones, theire welth to maynteyne.
"Whan[3] will the newe mone passe over", saie theie,
[margin: Amos: 8.] "And the Saboth that sell vitaile we maie",

480 "And make scaresetie of corne,[4] and the busshell lesse,
And sett up false weightes to deceive the nedie,
And sell chaffe for corne the poore to oppresse?"
This do theie which[5] are of riches gredie'.
'To amende', quod I, 'God make them spedie,
485 For if thatt prophett[6] nowe in Englande were,
His prophicie he shoulde se playne appere'.

'How[7] scarse withoute cause corne with us hathe bene,
Wherbie pore folke for lacke of breade did sterve.
The lyke derth in Englande was never seene!
490 Havynge corne inogh, the people to serve,
To fulfille the prophicie theie do nott swerve!
[margin: Corne maisters] For oure corne maisters yll councell did take,
Howe theie greate scarsetie of corne mighte make'.

[fol. 18r.] 'And further by theire vile covitousenesse,
495 When God dothe sende plentie of grasse and haye,
Theie are so gredie of worldelie richesse
Thatt theire cattell theie will not sell awaie

---

1 *Miche: 3*: Micah 3:2–3.
2 *To ... bones*: Micah 3:2–3.
3 *Whan ... oppresse*: Amos 8:5–6.
4 *corne*: grain.
5 *which*: who.
6 *prophett*: probably Ezekiel.
7 *How ... make*: this passage echoes PP A 7.183 and B 6.140.

Because with small cardge¹ then kepe them theie maye
To² gett theire owne price. Ought suche beastes to lyve?
500 No, nor shoulde not if I theire Judgement myghe gyve.'

'Yea', quod he, 'butt God³ to the shreude cowe doth lende
Shorte hornes, as tholde proverbe doth saie.
Butt I wolde advise England shortlie to amende,
Leste God by greater plages thake hir welth awaie.
505 Trulie, if aboundaunce did this lande decaie
For abusinge the same, what maie Englande thinke
That doinge as evill God will therat winke?'

'Aboundaunce of goodes, I thinke, to possesse
Is not the thinge that doth oure Lorde offende,
510 For theie be Goddes guyfte, geven of His goodnesse,
As He⁴ to Abraham and Loth did sende.
Goode are geven to all men', quod he, 'to one ende,
Butt if of those twayne theie wolde lerne goddes to use
Then shoulde not so many them so farre abuse'.

515 [fol. 18v.] 'For thabuse of aboundaunce was the cause part-
     lie
Of all this Contries hole distruccion'.
'Then', quod I, 'lett England take warnyng therbie,
For by Sathanas false seduccion
It⁵ hath therunto like introduccion.
520 Thoughte emonge the moste aboundaunce is small,
Yitt wicked possessours maie cause Engalandes fall'.

---

1   *cardge*: charge, load.
2   *To ... price*: to drive up the price of cattle by creating demand through scarcity.
3   *God ... hornes*: God gives the bad-tempered cow short horns [to cause less damage]. A common proverb; see Shakespeare's *Much Ado about Nothing* II.i.24 and Muriel Saint Clare Byrne, *The Lisle Letters: An Abridgement* (Chicago: University of Chicago Press, 1983), 49.
4   *He ... sende*: Genesis 13.
5   *It ... introduccion*: England has been led into this sinful state in a similar manner [to Sodom and Gommorah].

[*margin*: The fourth cause for the Sodomites fall was idlenes.] 'Nowe the fourth vice wherebie thies Cities did fall
'Was idelnes, the roote of all myschefe'.
'Did theie lyve'[1] quod I', doinge nothinge att all
525 That God therwith did take so greate grefe?
Then tell me playnlie for my wittes releefe:
Coulde theie lyve and do nothinge butt sitt still?'
'Yea', quod he, 'excepte theie[2] did thatt was yll'.

'Then tholde sayinge', quod I, 'in them trewe[3] was tried
530 whiche saithe when men do no godlie busynes
As[4] goode idle as not well occupied'.
'Truth it is', quod he, 'as thow doste expres.
Of to bad yitt better had bene idlenes,
Yitt ydlenes here hath not one respecte
535 For thosee thatt do – all are idle in effecte'.

[fol. 19r.] 'Then, alas' quod I, 'my fleshe quakes for fere
To thinke how many in Engalnde at this daie
Doth lyve as thoughe none other worlde were,
[*margin*: unlawfull games] And in vayne games doth spende the tyme awaie'.
540 [*margin*: Games used without gyle or for covitousenes are tollerable] 'Yitt', quod he, 'understand well what I saie:
Honest games mans mynde to recreate
I meane[5] not to be evill and clene[6] frustrate'.[7]

---

1 *lyve*: leave off, cease.
2 *theie ... yll*: 'what they did was evil'.
3 *trewe ... tried*: proved.
4 *As ... occupied*: neither idle nor well occupied, a common proverb (see George Latimer Apperson, *The Wordsworth Dictionary of Proverbs*, ed. Martin H. Manser [Ware: Wordsworth, 1993], 407).
5 *meane*: understand.
6 *clene*: truly, completely.
7 *frustrate*: destructive.

[*margin*: All games wherby man maie tryie his strenghte
God doth allowe] 'Some games be to man a helthfull
exercise,
And for the comon welth right commodiouse;[1]
545 Some that jentlemen oughte moste to practise,
In[2] feates of armes to be ingeniouse.[3]
Suche pastymes lightlie can not be viciouse,
Onles in the doinge a pride theie take.
The pastyme they maye use, butt the vice forsake'.

550 [*margin*: Thuse of all kyndes of artillerie[4] which maie be
fore defence of eny ralme is most lawfull[5] where the same
be by the lawe[6] permytted] Other games there be, to be
frequented
Of the Comon sorte for comon welthes gayne,
With whiche pastymes well done God is contended
Sith he willeth man comon welth to maynteyne.
Eche in his owne contrie, where he doth remayne,
555 For[7] whiche entent God gevith fort heire defence
In sondrie feates, sondrie experience'.

[fol. 19v.] 'Sith that is so', quod I, 'God graunte that I may
Se that in Englande men wolde exercise
Theire gifte geven of God to that ende, as ye saie.
560 [*margin*: Cardes, dice, boules and all suche like.] But many
other games theie rather devyse,
Neither good nor lawfull experince tries,[8]

---

1 *commodiouse*: profitable.
2 *In*: [so that they will be] in.
3 *ingeniouse*: resourceful.
4 *artillerie*: arms, not necessarily ballistic.
5 *lawfull*: permissible under God's law.
6 *lawe*: secular legislation.
7 *For ... experience*: 'To which end God provides [such games or exercises] for their defence through various achievements and different forms of knowledge.'
8 *tries*: produce.

At which many idle folkes that bene leue[1]
Thatt better occupied at home myght have bene.'

'Then', quod he, 'on[2] whome doste thou complayne?'
565 'I feare', quod I, 'all suche are not yitt knowne.
Thefore my complaynte maie theron remayne
Sith muche wicked seede thies gamsters have sowne,
For many false dice emonge them are throwne.
Ys not this thinke a kynde of idlenes
570 And muche worse', quod I, 'as I gesse?'

[fol. 20r.] 'Oh, good Lorde!' quod he, 'If all men did thynke
Of the straicte[3] accompte that eche man shall render
whan he shall approche evin[4] to the pittes brinke
Of eternall death. Unles he do tender
575 His soule helthe in tyme, and here remember
[*margin*: Math: 12.] That eche idle worde shall not scape judgemente,
He wolde beware how he the tyme myspente'.

'Alas', quod I, 'what wretched men are we,
which do not onlye by evill dedes offende
580 Butt in tyme, whan we moste devoute shoulde bee,
Thatt tyme of all tymes we do moste myspende?
[*margin*: Thabuse of the holie dayes.] The sondaie we shoulde oure lyves to amende,
Call for Goddes grace that we his will maye do,
Butt, Alas, I saie, we will not come therto'.

585 'For either theie will resorte to games vayne
Or go oute of the towne on the holie daie.
To come to the Churche theie do so disdayne

---

1 *leue*: indifferent.
2 *on*: about.
3 *straicte accompte*: full account.
4 *evin*: right up to.

[*margin*: Math: 7.] That perceyve[1] theire faith by theire frute ye maye.
In place of goode prayer theie do practise playe.
590 Of suche peoples lyvynge whatt maie we gesse
Is not suche doinges as yvill as idlenesse?'

[fol. 20v.] 'And worse, to', quod he, 'as comparison
Of two bad dedes together maie stande,
For all men are bounde of very reason
595 Oure Lorde God to serve on water and lande'.
'Yea, Mary!', quod I, 'but how is this scande[2]
To serve God all where bounde is every man?
Whatt nede we saie thaie to come to Churche than?'

'Upon this theire lewde libertie taken
God is not served as He oughte to be –
600 Perfecte devocion is clene forsaken.
More frome Godde service men did never fle'.
'Then the feare of God theie sett aside', quod he,
'An ydle life theie lyve, not regardinge
The workes that leadithe to lyfe everlastynge'.

605 [*margin*: Math: 20.] 'Whan[3] the husbande man wente forth, as Scripture showith,
To call worke men to worke in his vyneyarde,
He sett them then to worke of that that there growith
And eche to have a penny for his rewarde.
But if to his worke he have no regarde
610 And do the thinges there not mete[4] to be wroughte,
Thoughe he be doinge, yitt idle is he thoughte'.

---

1 *perceyve ... maye*: Matthew 7:16.
2 *scande*: interpreted.
3 *Whan ... rewarde*: Matthew 20:1–16, the parable of the labourers in the vineyard.
4 *mete ... wroughte*: supposed to be done.

[fol. 21r.] 'Me thinke', quod I, 'thies wordes soundeth not well.
Yf it chaunce[1] some men this sayinge to reede,
They will saie that obeyinge the Gospell
615 To obeie the Churche theie have no nede.
Youre wordes, theie will saie, therto doth them leede.
Theie doynge the workes mete[2] for the vyne yarde.
Other workes beside theie nede not to regarde'.

'The whiche dothe cause them that theie do neclecte
620 All workes by the Churche: to the comaunded[3]
Theie saie hir[4] preceptes are of none effecte,
Whiche of youre wordes maie well be gathered
Sith none other workes maie there be frequented
Butt[5] suche a vyne yarde doth apperteygne
625 All other workynge theie will saie is but vayne'.

'For the vine yarde dothe the Churche signyfie,
And workes to be wroughte there are Goddes preceptes pure.
And[6] to be bounde, say they, other workes to applie
Not comaunded us by the playne Scripture
630 To be done standith[7] in theire owne pleasure.
Therfore the Scripture theie followe, saie they,
And are no whitt bounde the Churche to obeye'.

---

1   *chaunce*: happened.
2   *mete*: appropriate.
3   *comaunded*: the binding teachings of the Church.
4   *hir*: of the Church.
5   *Butt … apperteygne*: 'except for such as belong to a vineyard'.
6   *And … obeye*: an attack against the Refored theological position of sola Scriptura and the Protestant rejection of 'unwritten verities', the teachings of the Church.
7   *standith … pleasure*: optional, not binding.

[fol. 21v.] 'To prove theie oughte' quod he, 'I will soone declare!

Did not Christe[1] to his owne disciples saie

635 [*margin*: Math: 23] Those[2] thatt dothe sitt, quod He, in Moyses chaire,
Looke what theie byd you do therto obeye,
Butt as theie do do in no wise ye maie
For hevie burthens theie bynde other to do,
butt themselves will not put a finger therto'.

640 'Were Christes disciples bounde by this precepte
To obeie the Pharesies or no? Lett them tell me'.
'Theie will say: "yea"', quod I, 'as longe as theie kepte
The lawe in theire mouthes, to this theie agre'.
'What[3] if in Scripture no suche preceptes be
645 As thei commaunded? Whatt saie theie than?'
'Mary', quod I, 'that soone aunswere theie can'.

'Theie will saie that those thinges theie disalowe'.
'Butt Christe', quod he, 'there makis none exception
Butt saith "whatsoever[4] theie do comaunde you
650 That do", saithe He, makynge no mencion
Of the lawe, butt to showe his meanynge theron.
"Theie[5] bynde hevie burdens to be borne", saithe He.
Thies[6] burthens thowe seilte the lawe can not be'.

[fol. 22r.] 'For the burden of the lawe God hym selfe bounde
655 And not the Pharesies. This theie muste graunte me.

---

1 *Christe ... therto*: Matthew 23:1–4.
2 *Those*: the Pharisees.
3 *What ... than?*: these two lines appear to be spoken by the narrator's interlocutor.
4 *whasoever ... do*: Matthew 23:3.
5 *Theie ... borne*: Matthew 23:4.
6 *Thies ... be*: 'These burdens that you have sealed cannot be the law'.

'Then[1] thoughe thies burthens were not in the lawe founde,
Yitt Christe worlde have them obeyed. Thow maiste see,
Then, if the Churche of Christe more parfecte be,
[*margin*: Thauctoritie of the Churche of Christe] She maie,
   as she dothe, suche goode lawes ordeyne
660 As to honeste lyvynge dothe apperteyne'.

'And all hir[2] children muche more bounde therto
Then all the Jewes to the Pharesies were,
For Christes Churche can will us none evill to do
Sithe by Goddes spirit she is ever ledde here
665 [*margin*: Joh:[3] 16 & 14] Into all truth, therfore it doth
   appere'.[4]

'And where as theie tooke a lewde libertie
Not to come to the Churche[5] materiall
With other to praie in perfecte charitie,
Because[6] all where to oure Lorde they maie call
670 (Whiche I graunte), butt yitt fynde this theie shall:
That Christe to the Jewes doth saie and declare
"My[7] house", saith He, "is calde the house of prayer"'.

[fol. 22v.] 'And nowe to come to my purpose agayne,
Those that in Christes vyneyarde sitte still
675 Or ells are doinge of dedes that are vayne,
   whiche may be in theire kynde,[8] neither goode nor yll.

---

1   *Then thoughe*: Even though.
2   *hir*: of the Church.
3   *Joh: 16 & 14*: perhaps references to John 14:6 and 16:13.
4   This stanza only has five lines lines. The rhyming couplet at the end appears to have been omitted.
5   *Churche materiall*: the physical Church with its human, sinning members.
6   *Because ... graunte*: 'Because God can be called on in every place, which I grant'.
7   *My ... prayer*: Matthew 21:13.
8   *kynde*: nature.

Yitt eche of those doubles[1] dothe againste Goddes will
And muste yeve[2] accompte of suche doinges all,
As of ydle[3] wordes Christe saith eche man shall'.

680 'Idlenes is a daungerouse thinge
   [*margin*: Eccle:[4] 333.] For, saithe the wise man, therof do-
      the ensewe
   Muche myschefe sithe there is no man lyvynge
   Butt beinge idell frome workes of vertue.
   The devill is redie his will to subdewe
685 To suche workes as maie the fleshe satiltie[5]
   As, for example, this a truth to trie'.

   'If[6] David the kynge had not idle bene,
   But had used some goode exercise,
   He had not Bersabee in the bathe sene,
690 The beautie of whome so shone in his eyes
   That his herte was enflamed. In suche wise
   Adultrie and murther therbie had successe.
   Suche is the daunger of this idlenesse!'

   [fol. 23r.] 'Nowe, as idlenes is in one respecte
695 Idellie to sitt still and do nothynge
   And many tymes comys to a wicked effecte,
      [*margin*: Omyttynge of vertuouse workes was a faulte
      emongest the Sodomytes.] So is there synne in vertue
      omyttynge,
   Whiche synne in thie cities was remaynynge.
   For besides thies whiche I have reherste,
700 Pitie on pore folkes theire hartes never pearste'.

---

1   *doubles dothe*: twice offends.
2   *yeve*: give, render.
3   *ydle ... shall*: Matthew 12:36.
4   *Eccle: 333*: Ecclesiasters 10:18.
5   *satiltie*: to thin or weaken.
6   *If ... successe*: 2 Samuel 11, the story of David and Bathsheeba.

"'For",[1] saithe the Prophett, "besides thies synnes all
Theie reached not theire handes to that pore and nedie",
whiche was an offence, thowe maiste here, not small.
Yitt worldelie goodes theie possest aboundauntlie'.
705 'Alas, if that offende God so', quod I,
'Englande hath greate cause to call for Goddes grace,
For trulie she maie matche this lande in that case'.

'Lesse mercie', I thinke, 'there was never seene
In all thies contries whiche so wicked were
710 Then is nowe in Englande, and late that bene.
Pore folke hath sterved for foode, farre and nere,
Because no mercie in those doth appere
Whiche had ynoughe theire pore neyboures to seerve.
Yitt like mercylesse men theie wolde se them sterve'.

715 [fol. 23v.] 'Butt wheare the Prophett doth note theire of-
fence
For not gyvynge almose,[2] to be so grevouse
In Englande, alas, we had experience!
[*margin*: Oure case is worse than the Sodomytes in
some respecte] That oure case therin in muche more
daungerouse[3]
For thoughe thies cities were moste viciouse
720 We rede not that they did pore menne oppresse
Nor made not the harboured[4] harbourelesse'.

'Nor pouled[5] not pore men by raysinge of rentes,
Or takynge of fynes, or incomes[6] so moche
As is nowe in Englande, which pore folk repentes
725 And shall as longe as there is eny soche.

---

1 *For ... nedie*: Ezekiel 16:49.
2 *almose*: alms.
3 *daungerouse*: grave.
4 *harboured harbourelesse*: create homelessness.
5 *pouled*: plucked, stripped.
6 *incomes*: entry and arrival fees.

Butt yf God, I saie, did thies with plages toche
For not gyvynge to pore folkes, whatt shall we saie
To those that dothe pull theire lyvynges awaie?'

'Trulie', quod he, 'God muste of His Justice
730 Plage those people, whatsoever theie be.
For, as thowe saiest, theire offence in this
Is before God muche more impietie
Then theie did comytte in this vile contrie.
Thefore if thei do not reprente and amende,
735 God will to them doubltes muche grater plages sende'.

[fol. 24r.] 'Alas', quod I, 'whatt wofull case is this
That men beinge never more worldelie wise
Then theie be at this daie, and well sene it is,
And knowith wherein oure moste myserie lies.
740 Yitt not one is founde that will exercise
Havynge witte joyned with auctoritie'.

' The cause therof', quod he, 'as I conjecture,
Is because themselves feare therbie to lose,
[*margin*: Private welthe is the cause that oure Common welthe amendeth nott.] And therfor for theire owne private pleasure
745 To amende this theie do nott themselves dispose,
Butt all thinges rekened,[1] I dare depose.[2]
Some[3] rente raisers therbie dothe not moche gett
If all thinges he buyeth to tholde price he sett'.

---

1 *rekening*: tally, account.
2 *depose*: attest, confirm.
3 *Some ... sett*: The sense seems to be that landlords who raise rent gain only little because his further acquitions are rented out at the old, lower price. The reasoning here is unclear, but the narrator may be thinking that a low rent is used to lure tenants who would not rent for a higher price.

'We do', quod I, 'butt caste stones againste the wynde,
750 For[1] this till God worke is paste remedie'.
'And Goddes workynge', quod he, 'ye shall nott fynde
Till man to Goddes grace this good will applie'.
'Then God graunte that to be shortlie', quod I.
'Lest God His grace agayne from us do pulle,
755 whose offer to us hathe bene so plentyfulle'.

[fol. 24v.] 'Amen', quod he, 'and graunte all Christen landes
To lerne by[2] thies Cities, thus punyshte for synne,
With prayer to oure Lorde to lyfte up theire handes
And to amende theire lyves, lovinglie begynne
760 That[3] the lande figured by this we are in
We maie at the laste daie fullie possesse
With God and his sainctes, the glorie endles'.

'Amen!', quod I. Than with that worde me thoughte
He vanyshed awaie, leavynge me alone.
765 Then came Morpheus, whiche me thither broughte,
And bad me not feare: 'Thoughe he was gone,
For thou shalte be where I found the anone'.
He had no soner spooke, butt I did awake.
Then home to my house my waie I did take.

770 Wheare this vision thus groslie I did write,
Voide bothe of lernynge, witte, and eloquence,
Requirynge the lerned, whiche can endite[4]
Suche matter more fyne, by theire experience
To pardon my fautes here where I make offence,
775 And by lernynge with favore the same to correcte.

---

1 *For ... remedie*: 'For this is a lost cause as far as God's work is concerned'.
2 *by*: from.
3 *That ... in*: 'That the land represented by this is vision is the one we are in'.
4 *endite*: write, craft.

For my will is goode, thoughe my witte I suspecte.[1]
FINIS

---

[1] *suspecte*: doubt.

BIBLIOGRAPHY

Apperson, George Latimer. *The Wordsworth Dictionary of Proverbs*. Edited by Martin H. Manser. Ware: Wordsworth, 1993.
Benson, Larry D. *The Riverside Chaucer*. Oxford: Oxford University Press, 1987.
Bradshaw, C. 'Huggarde, Miles (fl. 1533–1557)'. In *Oxford Dictionary of National Biography*. Oxford: Oxford University Press, 2004. DOI: 10.1093/ref:odnb/14049.
Byrne, Muriel Saint Clare. *The Lisle Letters: An Abridgement*. Chicago: University of Chicago Press, 1983.
Croken, Robert C. *Luther's First Front: The Eucharist as Sacrifice*. Ottawa: University of Ottawa Press, 1990.
Cummings, Brian, and James Simpson. *Cultural Reformations: Medieval and Renaissance in Literary History*. Oxford: Oxford University Press, 2010.
Doran, Susan, and Thomas S. Freeman, eds. *Mary Tudor: Old and New Perspectives*. London and New York: Palgrave Macmillan, 2011.
Dyboski, Roman, ed. *Richard Hill's Commonplace Book*. EETS OS 101. London: Kegan, Paul, Trench, Trübner, 1908.
Fletcher, Rachel. 'The Geometry of the Zodiac'. *Nexus Network Journal* (2009): 105–28.
Martin, Joseph W. 'Miles Hogarde: Artisan and Aspiring Author in Sixteenth-Century England'. *Renaissance*

  Quarterly 34, no. 3 (October 1, 1981): 359–83. DOI: 10.2307/2861491.

———. *Religious Radicals in Tudor England*. London: Continuum, 1989.

McCabe, Richard A. *'Ungainefull Arte': Poetry, Patronage, and Print in the Early Modern Era*. Oxford: Oxford University Press, 2016.

Richards, Judith M. 'Mary Tudor as "Sole Quene"? Gendering Tudor Monarchy'. *The Historical Journal* 40, no. 4 (1997): 895–924. DOI: 10.1017/S0018246X97007516.

Schmidt, A.V.C. *Piers Plowman: A Parallel-Text Edition of A, B, C and Z Versions*. Kalamazoo: Medieval Institute Publications, 2008.

Sobecki, Sebastian. *Unwritten Verities: The Making of England's Vernacular Legal Culture, 1463–1549*. Notre Dame: University of Notre Dame Press, 2015.

Walker, Greg. *Writing under Tyranny: English Literature and the Henrician Reformation*. Oxford: Oxford University Press, 2005.

Westbrook, Vivienne, and Elizabeth Evenden. *Catholic Renewal and Protestant Resistance in Marian England*. London: Routledge, 2016.

Wood, Andy. *The 1549 Rebellions and the Making of Early Modern England*. Cambridge: Cambridge University Press, 2007.

www.ingramcontent.com/pod-product-compliance
Lightning Source LLC
Chambersburg PA
CBHW070850160426
43192CB00012B/2377